The Ultimate Linux Survival Guide: Proven Tips, Tools, and Techniques for a Smooth Transition

By Ryan Nowack

Introduction: Why Even Bother With Linux?

You're in the middle of a game, you're right on the edge of victory—then bam, Windows decides it's update time completely distracting you causing you to lose. Or maybe you're editing a video, youre painstakingly lining up clips, when your software lags so hard you could swear it's buffering in real life. Or maybe you're just tired of your computer feeling slower every day for no good reason.

If any of that sounds familiar, then congratulations—you're exactly the kind of person who might love Linux.

Linux isn't just for hackers or programmers. It's for anyone who wants a faster, smoother, and more customizable experience without corporations breathing down their necks. Whether you're a gamer, video editor, or casual user, Linux can be a game-changer.

In this book, I'll show you how to install, set up, and use Linux without losing your mind. You don't need to be a tech wizard—I'll explain everything in plain English.

So let's get started and turn your computer into something that works for you—not the other way around.

Chapter 1: Linux, What the hell Even Is that?

If you've only ever used **Windows** or **macOS**, you might not have heard much about Linux. Or maybe you've seen movies where hackers type out mysterious commands on a black screen, making Linux seem like something only the truly advanced **tech expert** can use.

The truth is, **Linux is just another operating system**, like Windows or macOS, but with some key differences that make it faster, more customizable, and more secure. It's been around since **1991**, and today, it runs on **servers, smartphones, smart TVs, gaming consoles, and even the Mars Rover**. If you own an **Android phone**, you're already using a version of Linux.

So why don't more people use Linux on their personal computers? The main reason is that Microsoft and Apple dominate the market, with Windows holding around **69%–75%** of the desktop OS share, macOS at **15%–18%**, and Linux hovering around **3%–4%**. That might not seem like much, but here's the key difference: **Linux isn't pre-installed on most computers**, meaning that 4% **actively chose** to install it themselves.

But that doesn't mean Linux isn't a great option—especially if you're tired of slow updates, expensive software, and growing privacy concerns.

How Is Linux Different From Windows and macOS?

At its core, Linux **does the same things as Windows and macOS**—it lets you browse the web, edit documents, play games, and install software. The biggest differences are:

1. **Linux is Free** – No licenses, no subscriptions, no hidden fees.
2. **Linux is Open Source** – Anyone can inspect, modify, and improve it.
3. **Linux is More Secure** – Viruses and malware are much less common.

4. **Linux is Customizable** – You can change how it looks and works, unlike Windows or macOS.
5. **Linux Can Run on Almost Any Computer** – Even old laptops can run smoothly on it.

Feature	Windows	macOS	Linux
Cost	Paid (usually included with purchase)	Paid (included with Apple devices)	Free (various distributions)
Customization	Limited (some UI tweaks)	Very Limited (restricted UI changes)	Fully Customizable (can modify almost everything)
Security	Frequent target for malware (requires good practices & updates)	Strong (built-in protections, but not immune)	Highly Secure (fewer threats, strong permissions model)
Performance	Can slow over time (depends on system maintenance)	Optimized for Apple hardware	Lightweight and Fast (varies by distribution)
Gaming Support	Excellent (most games natively supported)	Decent (limited library, but improving)	Great (Proton, Steam, native Linux games, but some anti-cheat issues)

People switch to Linux because they're done handing control of their computers over to Microsoft or Apple.

What Are Linux Distributions (Distros)?

Unlike Windows, which currently has **two main consumer versions** (Windows 10, which is reaching its end of support in October 2025, and Windows 11), **Linux comes in many different versions called distributions (or distros).**

All Linux distributions share the same **Linux kernel** at their core, but they package software, system tools, and user interfaces differently. Some distros, like **Ubuntu and Linux Mint**, are designed to be beginner-friendly, while others, such as **Arch Linux and Gentoo**, cater to advanced users who prefer full customization and control.

Most Popular Linux Distros for Beginners:

- **Ubuntu** – The most popular, beginner-friendly option with lots of support.
- **Linux Mint** – Feels like Windows, making it an easy transition.
- **Pop!_OS** – Great for gamers and creative professionals.
- **Zorin OS** – Modern and sleek, designed to be user-friendly.

Think of Linux distros like **car brands**—they all have four wheels and an engine, but each one has different features and designs.

What Does Linux Look Like?

A common myth is that Linux is **just a command-line interface (black screen with text commands).** That's completely false.

Modern Linux has **graphical desktops** that look just like Windows or macOS. You can have a **taskbar, start menu, icons, and a system tray**, just like you're used to.

If you like the **macOS layout**, you can install a Linux desktop that looks like macOS. If you prefer a **Windows-style menu**, there are distros for that too. The best part? **You can completely change how it looks whenever you want.**

How to Try Linux Without Installing It

One of the best things about Linux is that you **don't have to install it** to try it.

You can create a **bootable USB** and test Linux on your computer without touching your hard drive. This is called **Live Mode**, and most Linux distros offer it.

How to Try Linux Safely

1. **Download a Linux distro's ISO file** from its official website.
2. **Use and download a tool like Rufus (Windows) or BalenaEtcher (Mac/Linux)** to create a bootable USB drive.
3. **Restart your computer and boot from the USB** (you may need to change the boot settings in BIOS).
4. **Explore Linux in Live Mode**—use apps, browse the web, and test everything.

If you like what you see, **you can install Linux alongside Windows** or replace Windows entirely.

Checking Your Linux Version (If You Already Have It Installed)

If you're already using Linux (or want to check which version you're running), you can find out with a simple terminal command. Open the terminal (**Ctrl + Alt + T** on most distributions like Ubuntu and Fedora) and run:

```
lsb_release -a
```

This will display details about your Linux distribution. If that command isn't available, you can also check using:

```
cat /etc/os-release
```

This will display information about your Linux distribution, such as:

NAME="Ubuntu"

VERSION="22.04 LTS"

ID=ubuntu

You can also check your **kernel version** (the core of the operating system) by running:

uname -r

This will show something like:

5.15.0-60-generic

These commands are **safe to run**, and they simply display information about your system.

Why Should You Consider Linux?

If you're **tired of forced updates, slow performance, or expensive software**, Linux is a great alternative.

Here are some reasons why people switch:
⬦ **No forced updates** – You decide when to update your system.
⬦ **No tracking or telemetry** – Unlike Windows, Linux doesn't spy on you.
⬦ **No need for antivirus** – Linux is much more secure by design.
⬦ **Fast performance** – Linux doesn't slow down over time.
⬦ **Fully customizable** – You can change every part of the system.

And best of all—**it's free.**

If you're ready to see what Linux can do, the next step is **choosing a distro that fits your needs.**

Chapter 2: Choosing Your Flavor of Linux

next step is choosing the **right distribution (distro)** for you.

Unlike Windows or macOS, which have only one version at a time, Linux has **hundreds** of different versions, all built from the same core. These versions—called **distributions** or **distros**—offer different features, interfaces, and optimizations.

Let's help you pick the best one for how *you* actually use your computer.

Why Are There So Many Linux Distros?

Since Linux is **open-source**, anyone can modify and redistribute it. This has led to the creation of many **customized versions**, each designed for different purposes:

- **Some are built for ease of use.**
- **Some focus on privacy and security.**
- **Some are optimized for gaming or creative work.**
- **Some are minimal and lightweight, great for older computers.**

Despite their differences, **all Linux distros share the same core system.** If you learn one, you can easily switch to another.

The Best Beginner-Friendly Linux Distros

If you're new to Linux, it's best to start with a **user-friendly distro** that works **out of the box**. Here are some of the most popular options:

1. Ubuntu – The Most Popular Choice

✅ **Best for:** General users, first-time Linux users, those who want a large support community.
✅ **Pros:** Easy to install, great software compatibility, lots of online help.
✅ **Cons:** Can feel bloated on older hardware.

Ubuntu is the **most widely used Linux distro**. It's stable, well-supported, and comes pre-installed with essential software. If you want a hassle-free experience, **Ubuntu is a great place to start.**

2. Linux Mint – The Best Windows-Like Experience

✅ **Best for:** Windows users looking for a familiar layout.
✅ **Pros:** Simple interface, pre-installed apps, good for beginners.
✅ **Cons:** Not as cutting-edge as other distros.

Linux Mint is based on Ubuntu but **designed to look and feel like Windows.** If you want a smooth transition from Windows to Linux, Mint is an excellent choice.

3. Pop!_OS – Best for Gamers and Creators

✅ **Best for:** Gamers, creative professionals, those using powerful hardware.
✅ **Pros:** Built-in gaming support, optimized for performance, sleek interface.
✅ **Cons:** Requires decent hardware, not as lightweight as other options.

Pop!_OS is **optimized for gaming, video editing, and other resource-intensive tasks**. It has **built-in support for Steam, Proton, and Nvidia drivers**, making it one of the best Linux distros for gamers.

4. Zorin OS – The Most Polished Windows Alternative

✅ **Best for:** Users who want a sleek, modern interface similar to macOS or Windows.
✅ **Pros:** Beautiful design, Windows-like interface, simple to use.
✅ **Cons:** Slightly larger install size compared to other lightweight distros.

Zorin OS is designed to be an **attractive, beginner-friendly Linux experience**. It's a good choice if you want a system that **just works** without too much tweaking.

5. Fedora – Best for Cutting-Edge Software

✅ **Best for:** Developers, users who want the latest features.
✅ **Pros:** Newest software versions, strong security, great for developers.
✅ **Cons:** Requires more manual setup than Ubuntu or Mint.

Fedora is used by many professionals and **even serves as the base for Red Hat Enterprise Linux**. It's a great choice if you want **bleeding-edge software and a secure system**.

How to Check Which Linux Distro You're Running

If you're already using Linux and want to check your distribution version, you can run:

```
lsb_release -a
```

Or use:

```
cat /etc/os-release
```

If you want a **fancy display of your system info**, you can install and use:

```
neofetch
```

These commands will show the **exact version of Linux** you're using.

Which One Should You Choose?

If you're not sure where to start, here's a simple guide:

- **Want the most beginner-friendly experience?** → **Ubuntu**
- **Coming from Windows and want something familiar?** → **Linux Mint**
- **Want a system optimized for gaming and creativity?** → **Pop!_OS**
- **Prefer a sleek, modern look?** → **Zorin OS**
- **Want the newest software and strong security?** → **Fedora**

No matter which distro you choose, **you can always switch later.**

Can You Try Multiple Distros?

Yes! Linux makes it easy to **try different distros** without committing.

1. **Live USB Testing** – Boot from a USB and test a distro **without installing it**.
2. **Dual Booting** – Install Linux alongside Windows and choose between them at startup.

3. **Virtual Machines** – Run Linux inside Windows using software like **VirtualBox**.

The best way to find out which Linux distro **works for you** is to try it.

You've picked a distro—now let's move on to **creating a bootable Linux USB**.

Chapter 3: Creating a Bootable Linux USB

Once you've chosen your flavor of Linux distribution, the next step is to create a bootable USB drive so you can try Linux or install it on your computer.

A bootable USB allows you to **run Linux directly from the USB drive** without making changes to your computer. This is called **Live Mode**, and it's a great way to test Linux before installing it.

Here's how to make a bootable USB so you can try Linux without changing anything.

What You Need

Before we begin, you'll need:

✓ A **USB flash drive** (at least 8GB, preferably 16GB or more).
✓ A **Linux ISO file** (the installation image of your chosen distro).
✓ A **tool to write the ISO to the USB** (we'll cover the best options).

Step 1: Download the Linux ISO

An **ISO file** (**Identical Storage Image** of optical media) is a complete copy of the Linux operating system that you'll install on your USB drive.

To get started, visit the official website of your chosen Linux distribution and download the latest stable version:

- **Ubuntu:** ubuntu.com/download
- **Linux Mint:** linuxmint.com/download.php
- **Pop!_OS:** system76.com/pop
- **Fedora:** getfedora.org

Make sure to download the correct version—**64-bit** is required for most modern computers.

A Weird Linux Distro That Runs from a USB

While most Linux distros are designed to be installed on a hard drive, some are meant to run **entirely from a USB stick**.

One of the most unique is **Slax**, a lightweight Linux system that doesn't need to be installed at all—you just plug in your USB and boot it up on any computer like a **portable operating system**. It's perfect for troubleshooting, secure browsing, or carrying your personal OS anywhere.

Even wilder? There's a Linux distro called **Damn Small Linux (DSL)** that's only **50MB** in size and can run on ancient computers. If you have an old machine collecting dust, you can turn it into a fully functional Linux system with **just a USB stick and DSL**.

Linux has something for **everyone**—from polished systems like **Ubuntu and Pop!_OS** to weird, ultra-lightweight distros that fit in your pocket.

Step 2: Choose a Tool to Make the USB Bootable

You **can't** just copy the ISO file to a USB drive like a regular file—it needs to be "flashed" so the computer can boot from it.

The easiest tools for this are:

- **Rufus (Windows) – Best for Windows users**
- **BalenaEtcher (Mac, Windows, Linux) – The easiest and safest option**
- **Ventoy (Advanced users) – Lets you put multiple ISOs on one USB**
- **Command Line (Linux users) – For those comfortable with terminal commands**

Step 3: Flash the Linux ISO to the USB

Windows: Using Rufus

1. **Download and open Rufus** from rufus.ie.
2. Insert your **USB drive** (make sure it doesn't have important files—you'll lose everything on it).
3. Click **"Select"** and choose the **ISO file** you downloaded.
4. Leave the default settings:
   - **Partition scheme:** GPT (for modern computers) or MBR (for older PCs).
   - **File system:** FAT32.
5. Click **"Start"** and wait for it to finish.

Once done, your USB is ready to boot Linux.

Mac & Linux: Using BalenaEtcher

1. **Download and install BalenaEtcher** from balena.io/etcher.
2. Open the program and **select your Linux ISO file**.
3. Choose your **USB drive** (make sure it's the right one).
4. Click **"Flash!"** and wait for it to complete.

BalenaEtcher works the same way on both **Mac** and **Linux**, making it the easiest choice for non-Windows users.

Linux: Using the Command Line (For Advanced Users)

If you prefer to create a bootable USB using the terminal, here's how:

List your drives to find your USB device name:

```
lsblk
```

1. Look for your USB device (it will usually be something like /dev/sdb).

Unmount the USB drive before flashing:

```
sudo umount /dev/sdX
```

2. Replace `/dev/sdX` with your actual USB device name.

Flash the ISO to the USB drive:

```
sudo dd if=/path/to/linux.iso of=/dev/sdX bs=4M status=progress
```

3. Replace `/path/to/linux.iso` with the actual path to your downloaded ISO file, and `/dev/sdX` with your USB device name.

Step 4: Booting from the USB Drive

Once you've created the bootable USB, you need to **restart your computer and boot from it.**

How to Boot from USB:

1. **Insert the USB drive into your computer.**
2. **Restart your computer.**
3. When the computer turns back on, **press the boot menu key** (usually **F2, F12, ESC, or DEL**—it depends on your computer).
4. Select **your USB drive** from the list.
5. Linux should now boot into **Live Mode**, allowing you to try it without installing.

Testing Linux in Live Mode

Once Linux boots, you can:

✅ **Browse the web** using Firefox or another pre-installed browser.
✅ **Explore the interface** to see how it feels.
✅ **Open the file manager** and look around.
✅ **Try the terminal** (if you're curious).
✅ **Check hardware compatibility** (Wi-Fi, sound, etc.).

If everything works well and you like the experience, **you're ready to install Linux.**

So, To Recap

Creating a bootable Linux USB is **the easiest way to try Linux without changing anything on your computer**. If you don't like it, just restart your PC, remove the USB, and your system will go back to normal.

Now that you have Linux running in **Live Mode**, let's move on to the next step: **Installing Linux on your computer**.

Chapter 4: Installing Linux Without Losing Your Mind

So, you've tested Linux in **Live Mode**, and you're ready to install it. Now comes the big question:

- **Do you want to keep Windows and install Linux alongside it?**
- **Or do you want to completely erase Windows and make Linux your only operating system?**

Let's go over both install options—and how to keep your stuff safe while doing it.

Step 1: Back Up Your Important Files

Before doing anything, **back up any important files** on your computer. While Linux installers are generally safe, mistakes can happen—so it's always good to have a copy of your documents, photos, and anything else you don't want to lose.

An easy way to back up files is to:

✅ Use an **external hard drive or USB stick**

✅ Upload files to **cloud storage** like Google Drive, Dropbox, or OneDrive

✅ Copy files to a **separate partition** on your hard drive

A Painful Lesson in Not Backing Up

A friend of mine once decided to switch to Linux after getting frustrated after switching to Windows 11. Excited to start fresh, he **skipped the backup step** and went straight to installation. He meant to **install Linux alongside Windows**—but in his rush, he clicked **"Erase disk and install Linux."**

In a matter of minutes, **his entire hard drive was wiped**, taking years of photos, resumes, work documents, and even his collection of abandonware with it.

Moral of the story? **Back up your files.** Even if you think nothing will go wrong, it's always better to be safe than sorry.

Step 2: Understanding Partitions (Don't Worry, It's Not Hard)

When you install Linux, your computer's storage is divided into **partitions**—think of them as different "sections" of your hard drive.

- **Windows primarily uses NTFS** (New Technology File System), which Linux can read but has limited write support without extra drivers.
- **Linux commonly uses ext4**, a modern file system optimized for performance, stability, and journaling.
- **Other file systems Linux supports:**
    - **ext3, ext2** (older versions of ext4, still used in some cases)
    - **XFS** (high-performance, scalable)
    - **Btrfs** (advanced features like snapshots, checksums)
    - **F2FS** (optimized for flash storage)
- **The swap partition (optional)** acts like virtual RAM when your memory is full, helping with system performance.

If you're erasing Windows, Linux will typically create these partitions automatically. If you're installing Linux alongside Windows, you'll need to manually **shrink a partition** to free up space.

To check your current partitions, run this command in the terminal:

```
lsblk
```

This will display your storage devices and their partitions.

If you're using Windows, you can check partitions in **Disk Management** by pressing **Windows + R**, typing `diskmgmt.msc`, and pressing **Enter**.

Step 3: Boot Into the Linux Installer

1. **Insert your bootable USB drive** into your computer.
2. **Restart your computer** and press the boot menu key (**F2, F12, ESC, or DEL**, depending on your computer).
3. **Select your USB drive** from the boot options.
4. When the Linux menu appears, choose **"Install"** (or try Live Mode again if you want one last test).

Step 4: Choose Your Installation Type

Now, the Linux installer will ask how you want to install it. You'll usually see these options:

Option 1: Install Linux Alongside Windows (Dual Boot)

If you want to **keep Windows and Linux together**, choose **"Install alongside Windows"**. The installer will:

✅ Automatically resize your Windows partition to make space for Linux.

✅ Set up a boot menu so you can **choose between Windows and Linux** when your computer starts.

✅ Keep your Windows files and programs intact.

This is a great choice if you **still need Windows for certain programs or games** but want to use Linux for everyday tasks.

Option 2: Erase Windows and Install Linux

If you want to **completely replace Windows with Linux**, choose **"Erase disk and install Linux."** The installer will:

✅ Wipe your entire hard drive.

✅ Create the necessary partitions for Linux automatically.

✅ Install Linux as the only operating system.

This is the best choice if you're **ready to fully switch to Linux** and don't need Windows anymore.

Step 5: Customize Your Installation

After choosing your installation type, the Linux installer will ask for a few more details:

✓ **Select your time zone** (usually detected automatically).
✓ **Choose your keyboard layout** (most people can leave this as default).
✓ **Create a username and password** (this will be your Linux login).
✓ **Encrypt your home folder** (optional, but good for extra security).

Then, click **"Install"**, and let Linux do its thing.

Step 6: Let Linux Install and Restart

The installation process usually takes **10-30 minutes**, depending on your computer's speed. Once it's done:

1. **Remove the USB drive** when prompted.
2. **Restart your computer**.
3. **If you installed Linux alongside Windows, you'll see a boot menu** where you can choose between the two.
4. **If you erased Windows, Linux will boot up automatically.**

Step 7: Updating Linux After Installation

Once Linux is installed, the first thing you should do is **update your system**.

Open the **terminal** (don't worry, it's easy), and run:

```
sudo apt update && sudo apt upgrade -y
```

This will:

✅ Download the latest security updates.

✅ Make sure your system is up to date.

✅ Prevent bugs and compatibility issues.

If you installed Fedora, use:

```
sudo dnf update -y
```

If you installed Arch Linux, use:

```
sudo pacman -Syu
```

✅ **All commands have been tested and verified to work properly.**

YOU DID IT!

Congratulations! You've successfully installed Linux.

Now you're ready to explore your new system, install apps, and customize it. Up next, we'll walk through how to make Linux feel like home by setting up software, drivers, and customizations.

Chapter 5: Making Linux Feel Like Home

With Linux up and running, let's make it actually feel like yours. At first, Linux might feel unfamiliar—especially if you're coming from Windows or macOS—but with a few simple tweaks, you can customize it to feel just right.

In this chapter, you'll learn how to handle essential first steps, like installing software, enabling hardware drivers, customizing the interface, and setting up must-have tools.

Step 1: Update Your System

Before doing anything, you should **update your system** to make sure you have the latest security patches and software fixes.

Open the terminal and run:

```
sudo apt update && sudo apt upgrade -y  # For Ubuntu, Linux Mint,
and Debian
```

If you're using Fedora, run:

```
sudo dnf update -y
```

If you're using Arch Linux, run:

```
sudo pacman -Syu
```

This ensures that everything is **up to date** and running smoothly.

Step 2: Install Essential Software

Most Linux distros come with **basic apps**, but you'll probably want to install additional software. Here are some must-have applications:

- **Web Browsers:** Firefox comes pre-installed, but you can also install Chrome or Brave.
- **Media Players:** VLC is a great all-purpose video and music player.

- **Office Suite:** LibreOffice is a free alternative to Microsoft Office.
- **File Syncing:** Install **MEGA** or **Dropbox** if you need cloud storage.
- **Communication Apps:** Install **Discord, Zoom, or Slack** for meetings and gaming.

To install an app, use your **package manager**. Here's how:

For Ubuntu, Linux Mint, or Debian:

```
sudo apt install vlc libreoffice -y
```

For Fedora:

```
sudo dnf install vlc libreoffice -y
```

For Arch Linux:

```
sudo pacman -S vlc libreoffice
```

If you're not comfortable with the terminal yet, you can also install software using the **App Store** equivalent for your distro (Ubuntu Software Center, Discover, GNOME Software, etc.).

Step 3: Install Hardware Drivers

Most Linux distros **automatically detect your hardware**, but sometimes you need to install additional drivers for things like:

✅ **Graphics Cards (NVIDIA/AMD)**
✅ **Wi-Fi and Bluetooth Adapters**
✅ **Printers and Scanners**

Checking for Missing Drivers

You can check if Linux detects your USB devices by running:

```
lsusb
```

Or check PCI devices (like Wi-Fi cards and GPUs) with:

```
lspci
```

If you're using an NVIDIA graphics card, you'll likely need to install proprietary drivers. The easiest way is through the **driver manager** in your Linux settings, or manually via the terminal:

For Ubuntu/Linux Mint:

```
sudo ubuntu-drivers install
```

For Fedora:

```
sudo dnf install akmod-nvidia
```

For Arch Linux:

```
sudo pacman -S nvidia nvidia-utils
```

Once installed, **restart your computer** to apply the changes.

Step 4: Customize Your Desktop Environment

One of the best things about Linux is that you can **completely change how it looks and works**.

Changing Themes and Icons

Most Linux distros let you change:
- ✅ **Themes** (how windows and buttons look)
- ✅ **Icons** (app and folder icons)
- ✅ **Fonts** (adjust text readability)

To customize these settings:

On **GNOME desktops (Ubuntu, Fedora)**: Install **GNOME Tweaks**:

```
sudo apt install gnome-tweaks -y
```

-
- On **KDE desktops (Kubuntu, Manjaro KDE, etc.)**, go to **Settings > Appearance**.

- On **XFCE desktops (Xubuntu, Linux Mint XFCE, etc.)**, go to **Settings > Appearance > Icons and Themes**.

You can download new themes and icons from www.gnome-look.org or your distro's theme manager.

Step 5: Set Up Useful Shortcuts and Tweaks

To make Linux more efficient, try these shortcuts and settings:

Essential Keyboard Shortcuts

- ✅ `Ctrl + Alt + T` → Open a terminal.
- ✅ `Super (Windows key) + A` → Open the app launcher (GNOME, KDE).
- ✅ `Alt + Tab` → Switch between open windows.
- ✅ `Super + Left/Right Arrow` → Snap windows to the sides (on KDE and GNOME).

Speeding Up Boot Time

If your Linux system **feels slow to start**, you can check which services are running at startup with:

```
systemd-analyze blame
```

This will show which services are slowing down your boot time.

Step 6: Enable Flatpak or Snap for More Software

Some apps aren't available in traditional package managers but can be installed using **Flatpak** or **Snap**.

To enable Flatpak:

```
sudo apt install flatpak -y

flatpak remote-add --if-not-exists flathub
https://flathub.org/repo/flathub.flatpakrepo
```

To enable Snap (Ubuntu already includes this by default):

```
sudo apt install snapd -y
```

After enabling Flatpak or Snap, you can install additional software from Flathub or the Snap Store.

Final Thoughts

At this point, your Linux system should be:

☑ **Fully updated**

☑ **Loaded with essential apps**

☑ **Running the correct hardware drivers**

☑ **Customized to your liking**

Linux is designed to be **adapted to your needs**—whether you want it to look and feel like Windows or macOS, or something entirely unique.

Up next, we'll go over how to run Windows software on Linux, including gaming and productivity apps.

Chapter 6: Running Windows Software on Linux

Switching to Linux doesn't mean you have to give up all your favorite Windows programs. Many Windows apps run **natively** on Linux, while others work through **compatibility layers, virtualization, or remote access**.

Need to run Windows software? I'll show you a few different ways—some work surprisingly well.

Step 1: Checking for Native Linux Alternatives

Before trying to run a Windows program, check if there's already a **Linux-friendly** version available. Many popular apps now support Linux natively, including:

☑ **Web Browsers:** Chrome, Firefox, Brave, and Vivaldi.

☑ **Office Suites:** LibreOffice, OnlyOffice, and WPS Office (great alternatives to Microsoft Office).

☑ **Media Players:** VLC, MPV, and Kodi.

☑ **Creative Software:** GIMP (alternative to Photoshop), Inkscape (for vector design), and Blender (for 3D modeling).

☑ **Messaging & Collaboration:** Discord, Slack, Zoom, and Teams.

If you still need a Windows-only application, the next steps will help you run it on Linux.

Step 2: Using Wine – The Easiest Way to Run Windows Apps

Wine (which stands for "Wine Is Not an Emulator") is a compatibility layer that **translates Windows software into Linux-compatible code**. This allows many Windows programs to run **without needing a full Windows installation**.

Installing Wine

To install Wine on your system:

Ubuntu/Linux Mint/Debian:

```
sudo apt update && sudo apt install wine -y
```

-

Fedora:

```
sudo dnf install wine -y
```

-

Arch Linux:

```
sudo pacman -S wine
```

-

Once installed, you can try running a Windows `.exe` file by right-clicking it and selecting **"Open with Wine"** or using the terminal:

```
wine program.exe
```

✓ **Wine works well with many Windows applications**, but not all of them. Some require extra setup or tweaks, which is where **Bottles** can help.

Step 3: Using Bottles for Easier Wine Management

If you find **Wine** difficult to configure, **Bottles** provides an easy-to-use graphical interface for managing Windows applications.

Installing Bottles

To install Bottles:

```
flatpak install flathub com.usebottles.bottles
```

Once installed, you can create **separate environments** for different Windows apps, improving compatibility and stability.

✅ **This makes Wine much easier to use for beginners.**

Step 4: Running Windows Apps in a Virtual Machine

If you need **full compatibility** for software like **Microsoft Office, Adobe Creative Suite, or certain enterprise applications**, running **Windows in a virtual machine (VM)** is the best option.

Popular VM solutions include:
✅ **VirtualBox** – A free and easy-to-use virtualization tool.
✅ **VMware Player** – A more powerful option with better hardware support.
✅ **QEMU/KVM** – The best choice for performance but requires more setup.

Setting Up a Virtual Machine with VirtualBox

Install VirtualBox:

```
sudo apt install virtualbox -y
```

1. Download a Windows ISO from Microsoft.
2. Create a new virtual machine in VirtualBox.
3. Install Windows like you would on a normal computer.

✅ This method ensures 100% compatibility for any Windows program but requires more system resources.

Step 5: Using Remote Access to Run Windows Software

If you have a **Windows computer** nearby, you can **remote into it** and run software as if you were sitting in front of it.

Options for Remote Access:

- **Chrome Remote Desktop** – Works inside a browser for easy access.
- **AnyDesk** – A lightweight remote access tool with good performance.
- **RDP (Remote Desktop Protocol)** – Best for connecting to Windows machines from Linux (`remmina` is a great Linux RDP client).

This method lets you use Windows apps **without needing to install them on Linux**.

A Story: How Valve Made Gaming on Linux Actually Happen.

For years, Linux gamers struggled with compatibility issues, forcing them to **dual-boot Windows just for gaming**. That all changed when **Valve (the company behind Steam) decided to invest in Linux gaming**.

Valve developed **Proton**, a modified version of Wine, which allowed thousands of Windows games to run seamlessly on Linux. Their work paid off when they launched the **Steam Deck**, a handheld gaming PC running **Linux (SteamOS)**.

Suddenly, developers had a reason to optimize games for Linux. Now, even major studios are considering Linux support **as part of their release strategy**, something that was **unthinkable a decade ago**.

This shift proves that Linux **isn't just an alternative** anymore—it's a platform that's gaining real industry backing.

Finding the Right Solution for You

There's no single **"best"** way to run Windows software on Linux. It depends on what you need:

✅ **Simple apps?** → Use **Wine** or **Bottles**.
✅ **Gaming?** → Use **Steam with Proton**.
✅ **Full Windows experience?** → Use **a virtual machine**.
✅ **Occasional use?** → Remote into a **Windows PC**.

Thanks to these tools, switching to Linux **doesn't mean giving up your favorite software**—it just means running it differently.

In the next chapter, we'll tackle something that **seems intimidating but isn't**—the **Linux terminal** and how to use it without fear.

Chapter 7: The Terminal Isn't Scary – Essential Commands for Everyday Use

If you've ever seen a hacker in a movie typing furiously into a black screen with green text, you might think the Linux **terminal** is something complicated and intimidating. But in reality, the terminal is just another way to **interact with your computer**—and it can actually make things much faster and easier.

This chapter will introduce you to the **most important Linux commands** in a simple, easy-to-understand way. By the end, you'll be able to **navigate your files, install software, and perform everyday tasks** without fear.

Step 1: What Is the Terminal, and Why Use It?

The **terminal** (also called the **command line**) is just a text-based way to control your computer. Think of it like speaking your operating systems native language. Instead of clicking through menus, you **type in commands** to get things done.

Why use the terminal?
✅ **It's faster** – Instead of clicking multiple times, you can do things instantly.
✅ **It's powerful** – Many advanced settings are only available through the terminal.
✅ **It works everywhere** – The same commands work on most Linux distros and even macOS.

✅ **It's not as scary as it looks** – You don't have to memorize hundreds of commands, just a few key ones.

To open the terminal, press:

- **Ctrl + Alt + T** (most Linux distributions)
- **Right-click in a folder and select "Open Terminal"**
- **Search for "Terminal" in your applications menu**

Let's start with the basics.

Step 2: Navigating Your Files and Folders

Just like you use **File Explorer** in Windows or **Finder** in macOS to browse files, you can use the terminal to do the same. Here are the key commands:

Command	What It Does
`ls`	Lists the files in the current folder.
`cd <folder>`	Moves into a specific folder (cd = "change directory").
`pwd`	Shows your current location in the system.
`cd ..`	Moves up one folder.
`mkdir <folder>`	Creates a new folder.
`rmdir <folder>`	Deletes an empty folder.
`rm -r <folder>`	Deletes a folder and everything inside it (use carefully!).

Example:
Want to go to your "Documents" folder? Just type:

```
cd ~/Documents
```

Want to see what's inside?

```
ls
```

Want to go back?

```
cd ..
```

Step 3: Creating, Copying, and Moving Files

Once you know how to navigate, you'll want to **create, copy, move, and delete files**.

Command	What It Does
`touch <filename>`	Creates an empty file.
`cp <file> <destination>`	Copies a file.
`mv <file> <destination>`	Moves or renames a file.
`rm <file>`	Deletes a file.

Example:
Want to create a new text file?

```
touch myfile.txt
```

Want to copy it to your "Documents" folder?

```
cp myfile.txt ~/Documents
```

Want to move it instead of copying?

```
mv myfile.txt ~/Documents
```

Step 4: Editing Files in the Terminal

Sometimes, you'll need to **edit text files** in the terminal. The easiest way is with **Nano**, a simple text editor.

To open a file in Nano:

```
nano myfile.txt
```

Once inside, type your text. To **save and exit**, press:

- **Ctrl + X** (exit)
- **Y** (yes, save changes)
- **Enter** (confirm filename)

✓ **Nano is beginner-friendly**, but Linux also has other editors like Vim and Emacs for more advanced users.

Step 5: Installing and Updating Software

Just like Windows has **the Microsoft Store** and macOS has **the App Store**, Linux has **package managers** that let you install software through the terminal.

To install a program (example: VLC media player):

Ubuntu/Linux Mint/Debian:

```
sudo apt install vlc -y
```

-

Fedora:

```
sudo dnf install vlc -y
```

-

Arch Linux:

```
sudo pacman -S vlc
```

-

To **update all your software**, run:

```
sudo apt update && sudo apt upgrade -y
```

✅ This makes sure your system is always up to date.

Step 6: Understanding Permissions (Why Linux Asks for "sudo")

Sometimes, when running commands, Linux will tell you:

```
Permission denied
```

That's because Linux protects certain actions from normal users to prevent accidental damage.

To **run a command as an administrator**, use sudo (Super User DO).
 For example, installing software:

```
sudo apt install firefox -y
```

Or restarting your computer:

```
sudo reboot
```

✅ **Only use sudo when necessary**—it gives full control over the system, including the ability to break things!

Step 7: Checking System Information and Performance

Want to check your **disk space, memory, or running programs**? Use these commands:

Command	What It Does
df -h	Shows available disk space.
du -sh <folder>	Shows the size of a folder.
top	Displays running processes and resource usage.
htop	A better-looking version of top (install it first).

Example:
To check how much free space you have:

```
df -h
```

A Story: How the Terminal Saved a Broken System

A friend once called me in a panic because his Linux laptop wouldn't boot properly. Instead of reinstalling everything, I told him to **open a terminal in recovery mode** and run:

```
sudo apt update && sudo apt upgrade -y
```

A few minutes later, his system was working perfectly again.

The **terminal is powerful**, and once you get comfortable with it, you'll be able to **fix problems, speed up tasks, and feel like a pro**.

Where to Go from Here

You **don't need to memorize** every command. Instead, focus on learning a few that **help you in daily tasks**, such as:
- ✅ **Navigating folders** (`cd`, `ls`, `pwd`)
- ✅ **Managing files** (`cp`, `mv`, `rm`, `nano`)
- ✅ **Installing software** (`sudo apt install <package>`)
- ✅ **Checking system info** (`df -h`, `top`)

As you use Linux more, **the terminal will start to feel natural**.

In the next chapter, we'll dive deeper into the **Linux file system**—so you know exactly **where everything is stored and how to manage it effectively**

Chapter 8: Navigating the Linux File System Without Getting Lost

If you're coming from Windows, you're probably used to **C:\ drive, Program Files, and My Documents**. But in Linux, things are structured **very differently**. Instead of a single **C:\ drive**, Linux organizes everything into a **tree-like structure**, starting from the **root (/) directory**.

At first, this might feel confusing—but once you understand the layout, it's actually **more logical and flexible** than Windows.

Step 1: Understanding the Linux File System Structure

Everything in Linux **starts from the root directory (/)**, and all files and folders branch out from there. Here's a simple breakdown:

Directory	What It Does
/	The **root** directory—everything starts here.
/home	Where **your personal files** are stored.
/root	The home directory for the **root (admin) user**.
/etc	Configuration files for the system and applications.
/bin	Essential programs (like ls, cp, mv).
/usr	User-installed programs and libraries.
/var	Logs and variable data (grows over time).
/tmp	Temporary files (cleared on reboot).
/mnt	Where external drives (USBs, external HDDs) are mounted.

✅ **Think of / like the trunk of a tree**, with all the other directories branching off.

To see this structure in action, open your terminal and run:

```
ls /
```

This will **list the directories inside /**, showing you Linux's core structure.

Step 2: Moving Around the File System

Now that you know what's inside the Linux file system, let's explore it using **basic navigation commands**.

Command	What It Does
pwd	Shows your **current location** in the system.
ls	Lists files and directories in the current location.
cd <directory>	Moves into a specific directory.
cd ..	Moves **up one level** in the file system.
cd /	Jumps to the **root directory**.
cd ~	Moves to **your home folder**.

✅ **Example:**
Want to check where you are? Run:

```
pwd
```

Need to go back to your home folder? Run:

```
cd ~
```

Want to list everything, including **hidden files**? Use:

```
ls -a
```

Hidden files in Linux **start with a dot (.)**—like `.config` or `.bashrc`.

Step 3: Finding Files Without Clicking Through Folders

If you ever **lose a file**, instead of clicking through folders, you can **search for it directly** using:

```
find / -name <filename>
```

Example: Looking for a file called `notes.txt`? Run:

```
find /home -name notes.txt
```

This will search only in your **home folder** (which is faster than searching the entire system).

Step 4: Checking Disk Space and File Sizes

Wondering **how much space is left** on your system? Use:

```
df -h
```

This shows **available disk space** in a human-readable format.

Want to check how much space a folder is using? Use:

```
du -sh <directory>
```

Example: Checking the size of your Downloads folder:

```
du -sh ~/Downloads
```

Step 5: Viewing the File System in a Tree Structure

Sometimes, looking at files in a **tree-like structure** makes navigation easier. If the tree command is installed, you can run:

```
tree
```

If you don't have tree, install it first:

Ubuntu/Debian:

```
sudo apt install tree -y
```

-
Fedora:

```
sudo dnf install tree -y
```

-
Arch Linux:

```
sudo pacman -S tree
```

-

Once installed, try:

```
tree /home
```

This will display your **home folder in a hierarchical view**.

A Story: How Understanding Linux's File System Saved the Day

A friend of mine once installed Linux and **accidentally deleted a system file** while trying to clean up space. Suddenly, **his computer wouldn't boot**.

Instead of reinstalling everything, I asked him to:

1. **Boot into a live USB** (a rescue Linux environment).

Mount his root file system:

```
sudo mount /dev/sda1 /mnt
```

2. Navigate to the /etc/ directory, where critical configuration files are stored.
3. Restore the missing file from a backup.

Within **minutes**, his system was back up and running—**no reinstall needed**.

Knowing where files live in Linux isn't just for organization—it can save your system.

Building Confidence in the Linux File System

At first, Linux's file structure might seem unfamiliar, but once you get the hang of it, **it makes a lot more sense than Windows' scattered folders**.

Here's what to keep in mind:

✅ **Your personal files live in** `/home`—**keep backups and stay organized.**
✅ **System settings and configurations are stored in** `/etc`—**don't delete things there!**
✅ **Use** `find` **to locate lost files and** `du`/`df` **to check storage space.**

Even with just a **basic understanding**, you'll be able to **navigate, troubleshoot, and manage Linux more effectively**.

In the next chapter, we'll take things a step further by **learning how to troubleshoot common Linux problems like a pro**.

Chapter 9: Troubleshooting Linux Like a Pro

Linux is incredibly stable, but **things can go wrong**—from system crashes to Wi-Fi issues. The good news? **Linux gives you the tools to diagnose and fix problems yourself.**

This chapter will guide you through **common issues**, **how to identify the problem**, and **the best fixes**—all in a way that's easy to understand.

Step 1: Diagnosing the Problem – Where to Start

Before fixing anything, **you need to identify what's wrong**. Here's a simple way to **break down troubleshooting**:

1️⃣ **Did the issue start after an update or installation?**

- If yes, try **rolling back the change**.

2️⃣ **Is the problem affecting only one program or the entire system?**

- If it's just one app, try restarting it.
- If your whole system is slow or unresponsive, **check system resource usage**.

3️⃣ Did you see an error message?

- Write it down! **Error messages are the key to solving problems**.

✅ **Pro tip:** If you're ever stuck, **Google the error message along with your Linux distro name** (e.g., *Ubuntu Wi-Fi not working*). The Linux community is huge, and chances are, someone has already found a solution.

Step 2: When Your System Slows Down or Freezes

If your computer is running slowly or seems unresponsive, **the first thing to check is resource usage**.

Check System Resource Usage

Open the terminal and run:

```
top
```

or (for a more readable display):

```
htop
```

(If htop isn't installed, install it with `sudo apt install htop` *on Ubuntu/Debian.)*

Look at:

- **CPU%** (If a process is using 100%, it might be stuck.)
- **MEM%** (If you're running out of RAM, your system will slow down.)
- **Swap Usage** (If swap space is maxed out, performance will suffer.)

Fixing a High-CPU or High-Memory Process

To **find and kill** a program that's eating up your resources:

Run:

```
ps aux | grep <program>
```

1. *(Replace <program> with the name of the app—e.g.,* `firefox`*.)*

Get the **PID (Process ID)** and stop it:

```
kill <PID>
```

2. *(If it doesn't stop, use* `sudo pkill -9 <program>`*.)*

✅ **Example:** If Chrome is stuck and slowing down your system:

```
ps aux | grep chrome
kill 1234
```

(Replace `1234` with the actual **PID** from the previous command.)

Step 3: Fixing Wi-Fi and Internet Issues

If you can't connect to the internet, first **check if your network card is detected**:

```
nmcli device status
```

If your Wi-Fi shows as **"disconnected"**, try restarting your network:

```
sudo systemctl restart NetworkManager
```

Then, check if you can **ping a website** to see if the internet is working:

```
ping -c 5 google.com
```

If that works but your browser still doesn't load pages, **clear your DNS cache**:

```
sudo systemctl restart systemd-resolved
```

 If the issue persists, reboot your system or check for missing drivers.

Step 4: Recovering from a System Crash or Boot Failure

If your Linux system **won't boot**, don't panic. Try these steps:

Check System Logs for Clues

If you can boot into **recovery mode**, check logs with:

```
journalctl -xe
```

This will show the most recent **system errors**.

Repair Corrupted File Systems

If your system crashes due to a **corrupt file system**, try:

```
sudo fsck -y /dev/sdX
```

(Replace /dev/sdX with your actual drive—usually /dev/sda1.)

✅ **If this doesn't work, boot into a Linux USB and run fsck from there.**

Step 5: Fixing Disk Space Issues

If your system is running out of space, check your storage with:

```
df -h
```

This shows how much free space is left. If a drive is **100% full**, find the biggest folders using:

```
du -sh /* | sort -h
```

Cleaning Up Large Files

To clean up unnecessary system logs:

```
sudo journalctl --vacuum-size=100M
```

To remove old packages and dependencies:

```
sudo apt autoremove -y
```

Step 6: Fixing Broken Software or Packages

If you tried installing something and now **your package manager isn't working**, fix broken dependencies with:

```
sudo apt --fix-broken install
```

For Fedora:

```
sudo dnf check-update
```

For Arch Linux:

```
sudo pacman -Syu
```

This should resolve most package issues.

A Story: The Mysterious Freezing Laptop

A friend of mine had an **old laptop running Linux**, and it kept freezing randomly. He was convinced Linux was **"too slow"**, but after a little troubleshooting, we discovered the real culprit—Since it was an old laptop from highschool **his hard drive was failing**!

How did we figure it out? A simple command:

```
dmesg | tail -20
```

This showed repeated disk errors, meaning the drive was struggling to read and write data.

Lesson learned? If your system keeps freezing, always check for **hardware issues first**!

Mastering Linux Troubleshooting One Step at a Time

Troubleshooting in Linux **isn't about memorizing commands**—it's about **understanding what's wrong and knowing where to look.**

✓ **If a program is slow or unresponsive, check system resources** (`top`, `htop`).
✓ **If Wi-Fi isn't working, check your network adapter** (`nmcli`).
✓ **If your system won't boot, look at logs** (`journalctl -xe`).
✓ **If disk space is low, check usage** (`df -h`, `du -sh`).

Even if you don't remember everything, **Google and the Linux community are your best friends**. Over time, troubleshooting will **feel less intimidating and more like second nature**.

In the next chapter, we'll explore **how to customize Linux**—from themes and layouts to making your system truly yours!

Chapter 10: Customizing Linux – Making It Truly Yours

One of the greatest strengths of Linux is its ability to be **completely customized**. Whether you want a **sleek macOS-like desktop, a minimal productivity-focused environment, or a flashy, animated Windows alternative**, Linux lets you build the perfect experience.

In this chapter, we'll cover:
✅ **Choosing the right desktop environment**
✅ **Customizing themes, icons, and layouts**
✅ **Hidden tricks and advanced tweaks**
✅ **Handy shortcuts and power-user tips**

Step 1: Choosing the Right Desktop Environment

Unlike Windows or macOS, Linux allows you to pick **different interfaces** (called Desktop Environments, or DEs). Each has a unique style:

Desktop Environment	Best For	Looks Like
GNOME	Modern, touch-friendly, minimal	macOS-like
KDE Plasma	Highly customizable, feature-rich	Windows-like
XFCE	Lightweight, fast, efficient	Classic Windows
LXQt	Ultra-lightweight, great for old PCs	Basic interface
Cinnamon	Traditional, polished, user-friendly	Windows-like
MATE	Classic Linux feel, lightweight	Traditional GNOME

Installing a Different Desktop Environment

To check which one you're using:

```
echo $XDG_CURRENT_DESKTOP
```

To install a new one:

GNOME:

```
sudo apt install gnome-shell -y
```

-

KDE Plasma:

```
sudo apt install kde-plasma-desktop -y
```

-

XFCE:

```
sudo apt install xfce4 -y
```

●

Step 2: Changing Themes, Icons, and Layouts

Applying New Themes (GNOME, XFCE, KDE)

You can change the system-wide theme using these commands:

For **GNOME**:

```
gsettings set org.gnome.desktop.interface gtk-theme
"YourThemeName"
```

For **KDE Plasma**:

```
kwriteconfig5 --file kdeglobals --group General --key ColorScheme
"BreezeDark"
```

For **XFCE**:

```
xfconf-query -c xfwm4 -p /general/theme -s "YourThemeName"
```

To **restore all GNOME settings to default**:

```
dconf reset -f /org/gnome/
```

Installing New Icon Themes

Want a fresh set of icons? The **Papirus** icon theme is popular:

```
sudo add-apt-repository ppa:papirus/papirus -y
sudo apt update && sudo apt install papirus-icon-theme -y
```

Apply it in GNOME:

```
gsettings set org.gnome.desktop.interface icon-theme "Papirus"
```

Step 3: Customizing Your Desktop Layout

Move the GNOME Dock to the Bottom (Like macOS)

```
gsettings set org.gnome.shell.extensions.dash-to-dock dock-position BOTTOM
```

To completely **disable GNOME's annoying hot corners**:

```
gsettings set org.gnome.desktop.interface enable-hot-corners false
```

Resize the XFCE Panel

```
xfconf-query -c xfce4-panel -p /panels/panel-1/size -s 32
```

Enable macOS-Style Window Buttons (Minimize/Maximize/Close Order)

```
gsettings set org.gnome.desktop.wm.preferences button-layout
':minimize,maximize,close'
```

Step 4: Customizing the Look with Wallpapers & Docks

Changing the Wallpaper

For **GNOME**:

```
gsettings set org.gnome.desktop.background picture-uri
"file:///home/user/Pictures/wallpaper.jpg"
```

For **KDE Plasma**:

```
plasma-apply-wallpaperimage ~/Pictures/wallpaper.jpg
```

For lightweight window managers like Openbox, use:

```
feh --bg-scale ~/Pictures/wallpaper.jpg
```

Automatically Cycle Wallpapers

Install **Variety**, a tool that changes your wallpaper automatically:

```
sudo apt install variety -y
```

Adding a Dock for a macOS-Style Look

Want a dock like macOS? Install **Plank**:

```
sudo apt install plank -y
```

Run it by typing plank in the terminal, then **add it to your startup applications** for a sleek look.

Step 5: Enabling Effects and Productivity Tools

Enable Wobbly Windows and Cool Animations in KDE

```
kwriteconfig5 --file kwinrc --group Plugins --key wobblywindows
Enabled true && qdbus org.kde.KWin /KWin reconfigure
```

Make Your Terminal More Useful with Aliases

Tired of typing long commands? Add **custom shortcuts** to .bashrc:

```
echo 'alias ll="ls -lah"' >> ~/.bashrc && source ~/.bashrc
```

Now, typing ll will list **detailed directory contents**.

Enable a Rofi Launcher (A Faster App Menu)

If your desktop doesn't have a great app launcher, install **Rofi**:

```
sudo apt install rofi -y
```

Launch it with:

```
rofi -show drun
```

Restart KDE Without Rebooting

If KDE starts acting weird, reset the desktop without restarting:

```
kquitapp5 plasmashell && kstart5 plasmashell
```

A Story: How Customization Made Linux Fun Again

When I tried Linux for the first time, I **hated how it looked**. I was used to Windows and found Linux "too weird." But after a coworker showed me how to install KDE Plasma, add a **macOS-style dock**, and apply **a modern theme**, I was Pretty blown away.

I spent hours **tweaking and perfecting my setup**—until I had a desktop that looked better than Windows and ran **faster**.

Lesson learned? Customization isn't just about looks—it can **completely change how you feel about your computer**.

Taking Your Linux Customization to the Next Level

Customizing Linux **isn't just about making it pretty**—it's about making it **work for you**.

✓ **Change themes, icons, and fonts** to match your style.
✓ **Use docks like Plank** for a polished look.
✓ **Automate wallpapers with Variety**.

✓ **Add shortcuts with** `.bashrc` **aliases** to save time.
✓ **Use Conky for system monitoring widgets**.
✓ **Enable fun animations like wobbly windows in KDE**.

Customizing Linux is **fun**, and it makes your system **truly yours**.

In the next chapter, we'll answer a **big question**: **Can Linux fully replace Windows?** Let's find out!

Chapter 11: Can Linux Replace Windows?

One of the biggest questions people ask when switching to Linux is:
"Can I fully replace Windows?"

The answer? **It depends.**

For most users, Linux **can do everything Windows can**—browsing, office work, gaming, media editing—but **some software and workflows** may still require Windows. The good news? **Linux and Windows can work together seamlessly** using different integration methods.

In this chapter, we'll explore:
✅ **Using Linux as your primary OS**
✅ **Running Windows apps on Linux**
✅ **Sharing files between Linux and Windows**
✅ **Dual-booting, virtual machines, and WSL (Windows Subsystem for Linux)**

Step 1: Can You Switch to Linux Full-Time?

Here's a quick guide to whether Linux can replace Windows for you:

Use Case	Can Linux Replace Windows?
Web Browsing, Office Work	✅ Yes, Linux is perfect for this.
Gaming	✅ Mostly, thanks to Steam, Proton, and Lutris.

Photo & Video Editing	⚠️ Possible, but depends on your needs (GIMP ≠ Photoshop).
3D Modeling & CAD	✕ No, many CAD programs are Windows-only.
Specialized Windows Software	✕ Requires Wine, VirtualBox, or WSL.

For **most general users**, Linux can **fully replace Windows**—but for those needing specific Windows applications, integration methods are available.

Step 2: Running Windows Applications on Linux

You don't always need Windows to run **Windows software**. Here are some ways to do it on Linux:

Option 1: Using Wine for Windows Apps

Wine translates Windows apps **to run natively** on Linux. To install it:

```
sudo apt install wine -y
```

To run a Windows .exe file:

```
wine program.exe
```

 Works great for many productivity apps, but may have issues with complex programs.

Option 2: Using Virtual Machines for Full Windows Compatibility

For apps that don't work well with Wine, run a full Windows **virtual machine** using **Virt-Manager**:

```
sudo apt install virt-manager -y

virt-manager
```

This lets you **run Windows inside Linux** without rebooting.

Option 3: Windows Subsystem for Linux (WSL) – The Reverse Approach

If you need **Linux inside Windows**, install **WSL** on Windows:

powershell

```
wsl --install
```

This lets you **run Linux commands inside Windows** without dual-booting.

Step 3: Sharing Files Between Linux and Windows

If you **dual-boot Linux and Windows** or have both OSes on a network, you'll want easy file-sharing options.

Option 1: Accessing Windows Files from Linux

Linux can read your Windows drive automatically. To mount it:

```
sudo mount -t ntfs-3g /dev/sdX /mnt
```

(Replace sdX with your Windows drive—usually /dev/sda2.)

Option 2: Using Samba for Network File Sharing

Samba allows **seamless file sharing between Windows and Linux**. To install:

```
sudo apt install samba -y
sudo systemctl enable --now smbd
```

To **create a shared folder**:

```
net usershare add myshare /home/user/shared guest_ok=y
```

Now, this folder can be accessed from Windows.

Option 3: Mounting a Windows Shared Folder on Linux

If Windows has a shared folder, you can mount it on Linux with:

```
sudo mount -t cifs //<Windows-IP>/SharedFolder /mnt -o
username=<Windows-User>
```

Step 4: Dual-Booting Windows and Linux

Some users need **both Windows and Linux** on the same system. Dual-booting lets you choose between them when starting your computer.

Setting Up Dual-Boot

1. **Create a Linux installation USB** using **Rufus** on Windows.
2. **Shrink your Windows partition** using Disk Management (`diskmgmt.msc`).
3. **Install Linux** on the free space.
4. **Let GRUB handle boot selection**—it will detect Windows automatically.

Best for users who need Windows for work but want Linux for everything else.

A Story: How Linux Saved a Windows System

In an It Course we had a test where we were given a **Windows PC that refused to boot**. The test being we have **important files we need to retrieve**, and Windows recovery tools **weren't helping**.

Luckily, I had a **Linux USB stick**. We booted into a **live Linux session**, opened the file manager, and **copied the files to a USB drive**—all within minutes.

Yes. And that's **one of Linux's biggest advantages**—even if you don't use it as your main OS, it can be a **lifesaver** when Windows fails.

Can You Fully Replace Windows?

For most users, **yes**—Linux can replace Windows. But for those who **need specific Windows software**, dual-booting or virtual machines offer the best compromise.

✓ **If you mainly browse the web, do office work, or game, Linux is great.**
✓ **If you need specialized Windows software, Wine or a VM can help.**
✓ **If you want both OSes, dual-booting is a solid option.**

Linux **isn't just an alternative**—it's a powerful OS in its own right.

In the next (and final) chapter, we'll discuss **what's next after learning the basics**, including how to continue improving your Linux skills.

Chapter 12: Your Next Steps – What to Learn After This Book

Congratulations! You've made it through the **Linux setup, customization, troubleshooting, and even Windows integration**. At this point, you're no longer a beginner—you're a **Linux user.**

But this is just the beginning.

Linux is a vast, ever-growing ecosystem, and there's always more to learn. This chapter will guide you through:
✅ **Where to go next**—advanced topics to explore

✅ **How to deepen your knowledge**—certifications, courses, and books

✅ **Getting involved**—contributing to the Linux community

By the time you finish this chapter, you'll know **exactly what to do next** on your Linux journey.

Step 1: Expanding Your Linux Knowledge

If you've mastered the basics, here's what you might want to explore next:

Topic	Why It's Useful
Bash Scripting	Automate repetitive tasks and system maintenance.
Linux Server Administration	Learn how Linux runs on servers and cloud infrastructure.
Networking & Security	Master firewall rules, SSH, VPNs, and system hardening.
Containerization (Docker, Kubernetes)	Understand modern cloud computing and DevOps.
Linux From Scratch (LFS)	Build a Linux system entirely from source code.

✅ **Where to start:**

Learn Bash scripting:

```
nano myscript.sh
```

```
#!/bin/bash
echo "Hello, Linux!"
```

Run it with:

```
chmod +x myscript.sh && ./myscript.sh
```

-

Explore Linux security:

```
sudo ufw enable   # Enables the firewall
sudo ufw status   # Checks firewall rules
```

-

Try setting up a **local server** using Apache:

```
sudo apt install apache2 -y
sudo systemctl start apache2
```

Step 2: Getting Certified in Linux

If you're considering **a career in IT or system administration**, getting a **Linux certification** can help open doors. Some top certifications include:

- **Linux Professional Institute Certification (LPIC-1, LPIC-2)** – A great vendor-neutral cert for proving Linux expertise.
- **CompTIA Linux+** – Perfect for IT professionals getting started with Linux.
- **Red Hat Certified System Administrator (RHCSA)** – For those working with Red Hat-based systems.

✅ **Where to start:**

- **Linux Journey** (linuxjourney.com) – Free beginner-to-advanced courses.
- **The Linux Foundation Training** (training.linuxfoundation.org) – Official courses.
- **OverTheWire: Bandit** (overthewire.org) – A fun, hands-on way to learn Linux security.

Step 3: Getting Involved in the Linux Community

One of the **best ways to learn** is to **engage with the Linux community**.

Ways to Contribute and Learn

- **Join Linux forums & Reddit**:
    - LinuxQuestions
    - r/linux
- **Help out on Stack Overflow & GitHub**

Try contributing to an open-source project:

```
git clone https://github.com/example/project.git

cd project
```

- **Attend Linux events** like FOSDEM, LinuxCon, or local meetups.

Step 4: A Story – How One Small Linux Fix Turned into a Career

A friend of mine once asked for help because **his laptop's Wi-Fi wasn't working after installing Linux**. He was ready to **quit and go back to Windows**, but I walked him through a simple troubleshooting process.

We ran:

```
sudo lshw -C network
```

And discovered **his Wi-Fi card was missing drivers**. Installing them was as easy as:

```
sudo apt install firmware-linux-nonfree
```

After rebooting, his Wi-Fi worked **perfectly**.

That moment made him **curious**—instead of quitting Linux, he wanted to **understand how things worked**.

a year later and he has a dual boot of linux on his desktop

The lesson?
 Your Linux journey can start with a small win—but it can take you to unexpected places.

Final Thoughts: Where Will Your Linux Journey Take You?

By now, you know:
 ✓ **How to install, customize, and troubleshoot Linux**
 ✓ **How to integrate Linux with Windows and run software**
 ✓ **How to keep learning and even start a Linux-based career**

Linux is more than an operating system—it's a **community, a skillset, and an open world of possibilities**.

Now it's your turn to **explore, experiment, and make Linux your own**.

 ◆ **Want to automate tasks? Learn Bash scripting.**
 ◆ **Want to manage Linux servers? Try setting up a local server.**
 ◆ **Want to contribute to open-source? Join GitHub projects.**

Your Linux journey doesn't stop here. **It's just getting started.**

Appendix A: Quick and Easy Linux Fixes

Quick Linux Troubleshooting

This section helps you fix common Linux issues quickly.

Wi-Fi Not Working?

1. Check if Linux detects your Wi-Fi card by running: `lspci | grep -i network`
   (For USB Wi-Fi adapters, use `lsusb` instead.)
2. Restart Network Manager with: `sudo systemctl restart NetworkManager`
   (If using a non-Systemd distro, try `sudo service network-manager restart`.)

Linux Won't Boot?

1. Try booting into Safe Mode by holding Shift during startup to access GRUB.
2. Open a text terminal with Ctrl + Alt + F3, then update your system using: `sudo apt update && sudo apt upgrade -y`
   (For non-Debian-based distros, replace `apt` with `dnf`, `zypper`, or `pacman` as needed.)

App Won't Open?

1. Launch it from the terminal to see error messages. Example: `vlc`
2. If there's an error, try reinstalling the app using: `sudo apt reinstall vlc -y`
   (For other package managers: `sudo dnf reinstall vlc` for Fedora, `sudo pacman -S vlc` for Arch, `sudo zypper install --force vlc` for openSUSE.)

Forgot Your Password?

1. Boot into Recovery Mode (select it in GRUB).
2. Reset your password by running: `passwd yourusername`
3. Reboot your system with: `reboot`

For more troubleshooting help, visit:

- AskUbuntu: askubuntu.com (Debian-based distros)
- Arch Wiki: wiki.archlinux.org (Arch-based distros)
- LinuxQuestions: linuxquestions.org (General Linux support)

Appendix B: Linux Terms Explained in Plain English

APT (Advanced Package Tool)
A tool to install and update software on Ubuntu, Mint, and Debian.

Bash
The command-line interface (terminal).

Bootloader
A small program that starts the computer and loads Linux (example: GRUB).

Cron Job
A way to automate tasks like scheduled backups.

Desktop Environment (DE)
The look and feel of Linux, such as GNOME, KDE, or XFCE.

Distro (Distribution)
A version of Linux packaged with specific features (e.g., Ubuntu, Fedora, Arch).

Filesystem
The way Linux organizes files and directories.

GRUB (Grand Unified Bootloader)
The boot manager that lets you choose between operating systems when starting your computer.

Kernel
The core of Linux that controls hardware and system resources.

LTS (Long-Term Support)
A stable version of Linux that receives updates and security patches for many years.

Mount
Making an external device (USB, external drive) usable in Linux.

Package Manager
A tool used to install and manage software, such as `apt` for Ubuntu/Debian, `dnf` for Fedora, and `pacman` for Arch.

Permissions
Defines who can read (`r`), write (`w`), or execute (`x`) a file.

Shell
A command-line interpreter that allows users to run Linux commands.

Swap Space

A part of the hard drive used as extra memory when RAM is full.

TTY (Teletype Terminal)

A text-based Linux interface used for troubleshooting when the desktop environment fails.

Wine

A compatibility layer that allows running Windows programs on Linux without a virtual machine.

About the Author

Ryan Nowack is an IT professional with over a decade of experience translating tech confusion into clarity. He's worked across Windows, macOS, and Linux systems, helping people navigate everything from everyday glitches to deeper system issues — all without drowning them in jargon.

He writes guides that feel like you're getting help from a friend who actually knows what they're doing (and won't judge your 57 open browser tabs). Based in Michigan, Ryan also dabbles in digital art, tech repair, and consuming way too much coffee.

Whether you're a beginner or just tech-anxious, his goal is simple: help you get things working — and help you understand *why* they work in the first place.

www.ingramcontent.com/pod-product-compliance
Lightning Source LLC
LaVergne TN
LVHW052321060326
832902LV00023B/4536